Praise

"In *Pieces of the World*, Nancy Crevier gives us a poet's tour of four distinct life arenas. Each contains a rumination about the earth, family, life as we know it and death as it comes to us. These are poems that soothe, that soften, that allow us to linger in the gardens of our days with the people and things that we love. Trees, flowers, mothers, lovers, aunts, mentors, God all make appearances here. But they are also poems that raise questions about how we face our lives, challenging us to see the beauty everywhere around us. At its core, these poems emanate a quiet kind of wonder and hope. After all, 'What more could we ask/Than darkness, gone?'"

  –Barbara P. Greenbaum, author of *The Last Thing*

"Adrift as we are in information, we seem to have developed insatiable and unhealthy appetites: tell us something we don't already know, even if it isn't true. Nancy Crevier's vital poetry tells us things we forgot we knew, things that are true, things both joyous and tragic that we need to understand to thrive as humans. And she does it with insight, compassion, and a depth of emotion words rarely approach."

  –Curtiss Clark, retired editor of *The Newtown Bee*

"You can't just casually read Nancy Crevier's poems... her words grab you and gift you with new insights when least expected. The poem 'Wedding Day' is wrenchingly beautiful and wise and should be required reading for every couple contemplating marriage. And for those who have been brushed by death and temporarily escaped, 'Cancer' is a gut-punch and a triumph. This is a beautiful collection of poems — every one to be savored!"

—Lea Embree, artist and museum exhibit designer

"Take your time, relish each poem in this book filled with images that evoke laughter, sadness, and an appreciation for life. Enter the world of Nancy's imagination and encounter revelation. Each of her poems is a gift to be unwrapped and enjoyed."

—Liz Arneth, retired English teacher

Pieces

of the

World

Pieces
of the
World

and other poems

NANCY K. CREVIER

Brush With Nature Publications

For more information or to contact the author,
visit www.ThePeachQuartet.com
or email info@thepeachquartet.com.

Book Design: Christy Day, Constellation Book Services
Author photo credit: Phil Keane, Blue Sky Farm Productions

ISBN (paperback): 979-8-9861938-2-3
ISBN (ebook): 979-8-9861938-3-0

Printed in the United States of America

This collection of poems is dedicated to the memory of beloved family members, and to all who make up pieces of my world.

AUTHOR'S NOTE

Where do poems come from? Even as my first collection, *The Peach Quartet and Other Poems*, was in its early days of publication, new poems were working their way into becoming *Pieces of the World*. Writing is a craft that bewitches me and surprises me. It is a process of self-discovery and discovery of the world around me.

Certainly, some of these poems are birthed in my own recollections. Other poems are blown in on the wind, as many seem given to me in just such a fleeting manner —I snatch them from the air before they disappear. I refer to other poems as "gifts from my muse." The worlds that spill from my pen are sometimes worlds apart from my past or current life, yet I encounter them as personal. Still others take their time, harvested from a place or moment, a bit of conversation, or even a word that slips pleasantly into my ear.

Only "Wedding Day" has been published previously by *The Newtown Bee* at newtownbee.com.

A good poem is like a good recipe: made up of ingredients that result in the best outcome, but that also allow for interpretation to suit one's taste. And like a good recipe, I hope my poems invite a pinch of thought, a dab of inspiration, and above all, smack of satisfaction.

CONTENTS

PART I
Murmurations

A MEMORY OF GARLIC

I think of you, my friend,
Every time I slip the skin
From a clove of garlic that you grew, dried,
Hung from rafters in your shed;
Great garlands that when you opened
The door, gathered themselves about your head,
A glorious crown that reeked of majesty.

Your hands reached up,
Released the strands, draped them in my arms,
Cupped my fists upon the bulbs
Pulsing with promise.

I raise my perfumed fingers to my face,
Inhale the residue of your generosity.

AFTER THE DROUGHT

Morning brings light subdued,
A cloud slung low upon the earth
Like the remnant of a dream.
Beyond sash and screen are colors hushed,
Leaves muted, blossoms veiled.

Fog
Drapes shrubs rendered shapeless
By summer's drought,
Cloaks clover now in silvery cape,
Bends brittle branches low — reveals itself:
A colorless rainbow
Caught against the skin of the sky.

My breath is a kiss on the window pane;
I press my ear against the glass, surely
Hear blades of grass — so parched they shiver
Beneath the sudden weight of dew —
Release a grateful sigh.
Then, rain.

From throats of flowers
Rise songs.

MURMURATIONS

In the yard we pause,
Rakes in hand,
The leaves' crisp voices
Suddenly silenced.

Treetops darken,
Blackened by starlings,
So many we cease to count.
Their calls ripple the air and as we stare
Bare branches shudder,
Shake off their burden
And the sky is raked by wing song.

We crane our necks to see the dance
At once magical and mad:
High then low then wide then narrow a band
Of syncopated movement,
Woven on the heavens.

Humbled, we move again
To clear our land;
Our rakes make clumsy patterns
In the leaves.

NASTURTIUMS

They are, this summer, a riot of lush leaves
And color — crimson, apricot,
A blush of coral blossoms:
These gems sunlit; and all of it
Spilled over stone walls and pathways, fragile vines
Twined about stems of nearby shrubs,
Nature's ornaments tucked in
Among the branches.

I shift the mass of green
To pluck one stem: bees rise
Buzzing with satisfaction
And I move on, satisfied as well.

PACHYSANDRA

We grasp green fronds and force the earth
To relinquish roots woven underground.
We employ hoe and adz, rakes,
And yank —

Pachysandra is persistent, resistant to our efforts:
Tamped down here it reappears
There and there and where it wants.
It wanders earthbound beyond the border
Creates a broader line of growth
Defies assault by shovel and ax
As if to ask what harm is caused
By greenery and flowery stems and if
This plot is not improved
By something so tenacious?

We pile high uprooted vines,
Rest our rakes, take off our gloves,
Reassess our struggle to remove
What once we wanted
But think we now despise.

FACES IN THE TREES

They watch us as we walk along —
Faces in the trees:
One-eyed monsters, googly eyes,
Squints and winks that freeze.
A grimace tries to be a grin;
A bulbous nose tops pointed chin;
A toothless mouth that forms an "O"
Is silent as it sees us go;
A smiling face frowns upside down
Beneath a twiggy, wild-rose crown.

I have a hunch that as we go
Tongues stick out and eyeballs roll,
Lips are licked and eyebrows raised —
But disappear beneath our gaze.
We shrug and nod acquaintance when
Bark and knots and holes pretend
That faces we see in the trees
Are only what we want to see.

BREVITY

The tulip has blossomed,
Exposed its center once
To the eye of the sun,
Opened its scarlet throat
To just one drop of morning dew;

But already it bows earthward,
The ethereal weight of petals
Heavier than the stem can bear.

It nods its head
Burdened by breeze;
I nod my head,
Let scissors ease its suffering.

KINTSUGI

Daylight unfolds in colors I could taste
If my tongue was not a silent rock;
If my eyes were not scattered in treetops
I could be enlightened.
If my hands were not seeking their fingers,
Feet, their toes —
I could go with the movement of night;
If my ears were not separated from my head
I could hear the breaking of dawn.

If I could dip my fingers in rivulets of gold
That seep through angled boughs
I could seal each crack beneath my skin,
Reassemble jagged edges:
Elevate perfection from within.

MERCY

There is beauty in the morning
When wind sweeps the memory of night
From the branches
And first light licks the leaves,
Plucks shadows from shrubs,
Rubs day's bright hands together
To ignite the dawn.
What more could we ask
Than darkness, gone?

THE COLOR OF WHITE

The sky is devoid of color today.
We forget that blue ever existed
Or gray.
We cannot remember the play of clouds
Tinged with pink and yellow.
Our eyes seek to expose a break
In the bleak expanse.

Yesterday the sunset consumed the roses
And daylilies.

The absence of color is heavy
In this white world.

EARTHQUAKE

Giants below us rumble and roar,
Grumble and growl,
Wake up and prowl 'neath Earth's hot core.

They burp and fart, they toss and turn
Till giant arms emerge and rise,
Churn the ground, split moss from ferns.

With giant hands they shake the shrubs,
Make birds' nests shudder, and mountains fall;
Pry boulders wide, heave rocks from walls.

Giant feet kick up their heels
Till timbers crack and hillsides reel;
Rattle rocks and reroute rivers,
Leave canyons, valleys all aquiver.

Giant shoulders shrug aside
Mammoth glaciers, canyons, cliffs;
Crumple vistas, split stones wide.
Sky and ground reverberate
As every movement recreates.

Then giants yawn and fall asleep
In hollow spaces dark and deep.
Giant eyes are closed at last,
Ruckus calmed and quickly past.
Reconstructed at their will
The world revolves, begins to heal.

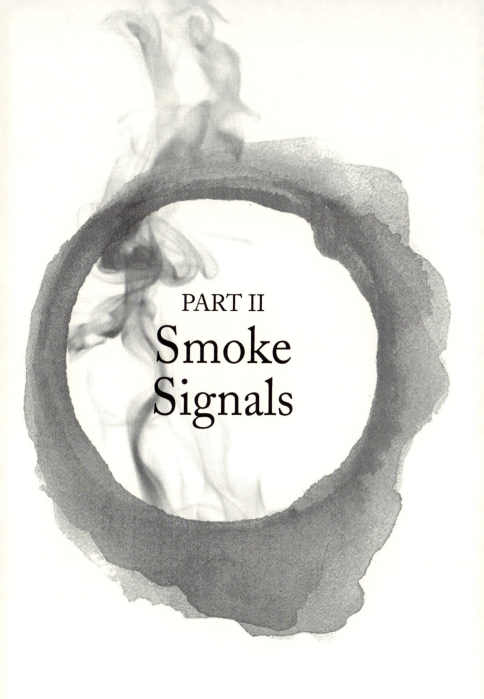

PART II
Smoke
Signals

AUNT DOROTHY DANCING

Thanksgiving, c. 1960

You will be forever forty
Dancing in your mother's kitchen.
The turkey, long plucked free
Of bothersome pinfeathers,
Long plucked free of flesh;
Its skeletal remains rest upon the counter
While you,
Eyes bright and snapping
Flecks of green,
Slap and flick the dish towel.
You lean toward me with music in your mouth,
Lips so red
Beneath the blaze of the bare bulb
Above our heads.
I am swept away in your holiday waltz,
The worn linoleum crackling
Beneath our feet,
While my mother and yours
Pile high plates that will bounce on back seats
Homeward bound.

ARDIS

I think of my grandmother, steeped in Catholicism,
Entrenched in Midwestern ways,
Who christened her children with common names:
Except my mother whose name was other,
Whose name was a melody sung by flowers.
She saw the child in need of a name
As beautiful as it was strange; a name of strength,
A name with the fervor of a rushing river.

I think of my grandmother, eighth grade enough
For a girl so wise, with a face so sweet
She could marry well; well bred, well read;
And wonder why
This French woman in a Norwegian bed
Graced her third of four children
With a name that when held to her lips
Quenched her thirst like the first sip of stout
On a hot summer day,
That left a taste of Ireland in her mouth.

Maybe "Ardis" was whispered in her ear,
Maybe nurtured in her heart, maybe ripened finally
In the belly of winter.
Maybe "Ardis" was written on the palm of December,
Pressed to her own, pressed to the forehead
Of the babe in her arms.

I think of my grandmother, immersed in tradition,
Emboldened enough to raise the priest's eyebrows,
To bless my mother
With every damp cross at the baptismal font.

SMOKE SIGNALS

My great-aunt counted coins,
Plucked preciousness from her purse,
Reminded me as each one clinked to the tabletop
Their worth.

But when snow transformed her yard
And thermometers shivered
Far below zero,
She put no price on seeds
To feed the flocks that stayed
In blue and gray of January,
Flecks of color on frozen earth.

Seated at her kitchen table
We watched birds gather,
Our eyes hidden behind binoculars
Until seeds disappeared; then
My great-aunt would move down steps
More hidden than seen by drifts of snow,
Step-slide her way to replace the feast.

Seeds spilled from her bucket,
Rained about her like a strange winter storm,
Mingled with smoke of her cigarette
Clasped tightly in lips split by years and cold —
Every handful of seeds an extravagance.
Then the same step-slide to shrouded steps,

Hand over hand on the wooden rail —
A Mount Everest in Minnesota;
Returned to the sharp, steamy presence
Of a wood-burning stove,
Shook seeds from cuffs, unfurled shawl.

My great-aunt counted birds
As precious as her coins,
Showed me their worth,
The value of beauty.

The smoke from her cigarette was a halo
Encircling her head.

BIG SISTER

I remember when you taught me
To catch:
My hands outstretched —
You just a step away,
Your toss a gentle play between us.

You clapped when my small arms
Clasped the ball,
Crushed it close to my chest;
You did not rest but moved back a step,
Then reached toward me.

I threw the ball —
My enthusiasm too much
To make it fall
Where you could snatch it from the air;
But you laughed and cheered.

We started over:
You one step forward,
My hands outstretched
Until I could catch and throw
Well enough to move us into the future.

TENDER LIES

My father hid his broken heart,
Did not tell my mother when they met
That the flutter he felt
Was more than wings of love
Beating within his rib cage.

Her lovely face, he said,
Erased the pain of each heartbeat,
Softened scars left by damaged love —
The deeper damage unacknowledged
In their marriage bed.

He layered lies between sweet words
And cold sweats,
Medicine slipped between sips of beer —
Her juicy lips unaware.

His hands on her hips made promises
He could not keep, would not share the rest:
That the swell of his heart was more
Than the poet's tale of true love
Destined to explode, his hand
Held close to his chest.

My father fashioned fiction
For my mother,

Did not tell her each skipped beat
Was more than passion:
That a heart overwhelmed by love
Could burst.

FOR A POET

For S.E.

In the yellow house
For over half a century, yours,
You sit at the table,
Surrounded by paper, pens, and flowers,
A dog of some age at your feet.
Beyond the sliding glass doors
Is what you will create.

You will watch the winter wind
Sweep away autumn in one snowy stroke,
Hide the yard beneath smooth plains
Of white;
You will write the story of today.

You will watch as buds swell
And tell of springtime well underway
As it layers the lawn in shades of yellow
And green;
You will write all you have seen today.

You will watch summer sun
Chase thunderclouds, paint rainbows,
Cast shadows on shrubs and blossoms
Now bright;
You will write the day's beauty today.

You will watch autumn swap colors
With earth and trees,
Marvel at sparkle of hoar frost on branches,
Silvery glow.
You will write of faded glory today.

In the yellow house, yours,
A half century of observation measured
Season by season;
You set down pen and pet
A dog of some age at your feet.

TO MY CAT

While the piano sings beneath someone's fingers
In another room,
I whisper bedtime poems to you,
Nestled at my knees:
Mary Oliver, Emily Dickinson,
And lately, Walt Whitman.

Your gold eyes open and shut
Keeping time with the rhyme and words
Of each stanza.
Your ears flick, like a beat poet's click of the fingers
I take to be appreciative.

You have your favorites, I imagine,
Mary's dog poems, Walt's elegy of nature,
Emily's fly buzzing so loudly
That you stare suddenly skyward,
Seek that fly, but not the death it portends.

I pretend that you are rapt,
Though often before final phrases
Crawl across rumpled covers,
Before I finish with a flourish,
You have abandoned the literary moment
To stalk the night hallways,
Leave me to whisper to myself,
My fingers caught in the pages.

BENEATH THE SURFACE

X-rays reveal to expert eyes
What others cannot see:
Van Gogh's face, faint,
Behind the portrait of a woman,
Behind a hundred years of paint —
The image of the artist, a discard.

The canvas turned, precious paint applied;
The artist's gaze turned inward, hides
Behind this peasant face,
Not easily uncovered, nor erased.

Your expert eyes turn inward
See what others cannot see
Behind a pleasant face:
What is concealed
Beneath endless years of pain —
Your image, undiscovered.

THE WOMAN IN THE GIFT SHOP

The woman in the gift shop seeks
What is not there.
The couture bag slung over her shoulder
Is heavy with the weight of want.
Disappointment trails her, lingers
In aisles while she assesses
What could be hers.

Our eyes meet framed by shelves,
Veiled by objects of questionable desire;
And when our hands wrap about
The same strand of polished stones
And silver I loosen my grip:
Feel her need exceeds my own.

A MOMENT IN THE PARK

The old man perches on a bench
As if he might take flight,
Or rise to where a wren nearby
Is balanced on a branch,
Poised, nearly alight.

The park is music and voices,
A choice word heard could frighten
Either one.
Eyes flicker, breath halts
At what might be beyond their sights.

The old man inches forward,
Hips hover, finger points skyward
Though the wren remains:
A furtive glance notes the gesture.

The bench tips forward,
The branch bends, then
It is the wren that takes measure,
Lifts and leaves.

The old man edges back.
Where did it go? he asks.
I have no answer.
A feather drifts past his outstretched hand.

LATECOMER

The chicken lady squawks
From the back of the room —
Wants to talk about her work,
Pecks at poems she has not heard,
Takes to task words and their worth.

She wades in her own shit,
Waits for me to point to it or
Scatter grains of information
For her to scratch.

She thinks the patter of applause
Is hers to take,
Rakes in the chatter
Like she is turning up dirt.

When I tire of hearing her cluck
About her bad luck and lofty airs
I smile, point to the clock
Ticking toward the end of time
Just like the patient fox
Outside the coop.

NEIGHBORS

The fox behind our houses
Is a surprise:
A rhythmic flow back and forth —
A feral pendulum —
Forced by borders it has set
To turn and return, side to side,
Heedless of our inside eyes.

Its movement is steadfast
Though I cannot tell if that might be
To drive crazy the dog, inside,
Hampered from pursuit
By walls and windows,
Or if it is mole or mouse
Sought to carry back to that stone wall
Or broken branched lean-to
That mark the lines
Between what is ours and yours.

This vixen — or reynard — appears, disappears
Behind the shelter of our tool shed, reappears
Where your trees shake hands with mine.
I am mesmerized —
It does not halt nor pause its pace.
I wonder if you wonder, too, if it simply moves
To prove whose woods these are:
Or just to tease the dog, inside.

If you and I should rise
From our chairs, open our doors;
If you should step forward and my dog race forth,
What would be the worth of that?
Its startled look framed,
Our wooded boundaries reclaimed
With its frightened sprint;
And the dog's piss
Crackling the leaves as it flees?

I trace its passage between our yards,
Its grace this morning's gift, a grin —
Or grimace — on its forward pointed face.
The dog drools, my hand falls
From the door knob.
I call you to say, "Don't move."

To rob this moment of its beauty
Would be a keen disappointment.

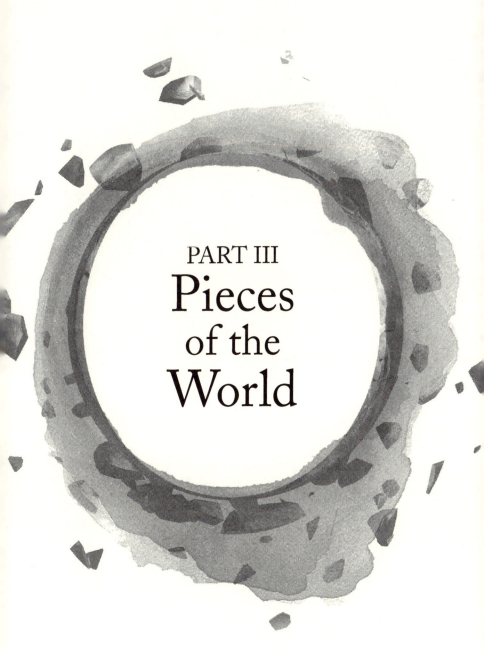

PART III
Pieces
of the
World

POEMS FROM THE PEW

This is my confession:
While you preach I pray
To my muse,
Amuse myself with words that rhyme,
Time to time incorporating what you say
Into phrases I will carry home in my head,
Place them on paper, hope that they are read.

Your stories are fodder for all I need:
Feed my fantasies with peace and love
And angels above us, their heads in the clouds
Much as are mine as I whisper aloud
The prayers and invocations, sing hymns
While the rhythm of a new verse
Crowds your message, dims your words.

I could apologize:
You do not know that when you speak
I close my eyes
To better hear the voices
Instead of verses you have crafted.
After the service I slip out,
Let a raft of new thoughts grant absolution,
Wait for benediction.

SUMMER POW WOW

The ceremony just over the field
Where in the grandstand earlier that day
My white face, blue eyes
Denied any heritage.
Brown skin, black eyes held my gaze.

My pale hands fingered fry bread,
My throat searched the thread of connection;
I waited for the drum to call my name.
I could sense the strike of stick on skin
Stretched as tightly as my own,
The bones of the drum as distinct as those
That molded my frame.
I sat close to the drummers, hoarded their song
To carry home.

Wide open window on the summer night,
I heard the drumbeat in my chest,
A second heart to mirror my own,
Steady strokes that spoke to my blood
Even while they shook me
Nestled in a child's bed, used to cricket song
And muffled voices behind closed doors.
I listened and felt the jingle dress dance
Burn in my soles,
My soul catch fire.

RESTAURANT LORE

Kitchen prep taught me
Rule one: To have on hand the things I love
Rule two: All in proper place;
Rule three: To time the dance from stove to plate,
Rule four: To guesstimate the who and what
Of guests that grace our tables.

Kitchen prep taught me
Rule five: To never waste what could be used
Rule six: To recreate, invent;
Rule seven: To sweep clean today's chaos
To avoid tomorrow's sorrow.

Kitchen prep prepared me
Rule eight: For what goes wrong when in the weeds —
See rule one:
It did not spare me the cupboard bare,
The things I most loved
Abandoned.

TO ROCK A CRADLE

I am wrapping baby gifts:
Presents of hope,
Tokens of resilience
Of which I am envious — and not.

I fold tapered ends of paper
Up, tape them in place;
Wonder if faces will curl
Up, like the bows, smiles
Of blissful ignorance?

The strength it takes to rock a cradle
Is Herculean in this ever-shifting world.

PIECES OF THE WORLD

We do not differ from the smallest bird,
The least whisper, the shortest night.

We are not more than the wave
Pressed upon the shoreline,
Not stronger than clouds
That eclipse burning stars.

We are not more than the movement of earth,
Or the sound of pebbles rolled beneath footsteps;
We are not greater than the wing feather
Of a dove or the beat of a butterfly's heart.

Each transformation jars the universe,
Sends a shiver through the galaxy.

WALKING THE DOG

Morning has not yet entered the houses we pass,
Nor the one we left behind.
First light finds only our footprints
In blue shadows and new fallen snow.
Our breath curls back upon itself
A frozen palm pressed against our mouths
To protect a perfect silence.

Our legs — your four, my two —
Shake off sleep slowly; our pace
Interrupted by your nose for news
Deposited on frosted grass,
By my gaze at Christmas lights muted
By mantles of snow.

Behind dark windows we do not know
Who sleeps or watches from lightless rooms;
Doors shut tight shun this morning's light.
Do dogs within chase yesterday's squirrels
With quivering feet, slumber still curled small
As we walk by, unaware of the greeting
You leave steaming on this street?

We hurry now, our legs alive:
There is much that we must do.
When we return to where we started
The kitchen light runs down the steps
To welcome us home.

SINCE YOU ASK

Here is what I recall:
When snow fell
Before fall gave way to winter,
Drifts so deep the effort
Brought us laughing to our knees;

When we arose we posed
Like white angels we were not,
Collapsed again, waved arms and legs
To burn our images in ice —
Left the illusion that here
Had passed seraphim;
Lobbed orbs of crystal snow that burst
Like falling stars through frigid air.
And snow kept falling.

Here is what I recall:
Sled runners traced on white hills
Falling downward;
We were tangled arms and legs
A hilarious heap of humanity
Humbled by the snowbank at the bottom
That bucked us from our rides,
Frost on our faces a taste of heaven.

The toboggan heaved upright —
We scrambled to the top again even
As sunlight hastened to the horizon,
Left only purple shadows to mark the way home.
When we looked back, our footsteps were memories.
And snow kept falling.

Here is what I recall:
There was always snow and your kiss
A chapped promise of love
Left on my lips at the doorway.

ADRIFT

While you drift in dreams
I move toward morning,
No longer moored to our bed,
Pulled to witness
Night undress its darkness,
Divulge the day
In shades of blue.

While I linger, fingers pressed
Against the pane,
I hear you stir, watch you reach
For me. Forgive me:
I am anchored here,
Unable to return.

When the horizon glows
The color of your cheeks caught
By winter's breath —
I catch mine.

WEDDING DAY

Do not squander love on just one day;
Savor its largeness, hoard some for a time
When it seems far away
From promises made,
As faded as the corsage
Crushed on a lapel.

Do not waste the wealth of love on these few hours,
Cherish its fullness, gather some close
To let loose when it flounders
And this day feels lost,
A mark on the calendar
That might be erased.

Do not give all of love this day;
Treasure its immensity, save some
Should jealousy occlude the eyes
With heavy veil
That will not easily
Be thrust aside.

This moment longs to lavish love,
To shake every drop from the vessel
Of the heart;
Keep a reservoir to draw upon
To ease an unexpected thirst,
One into which you can thrust your hands,

Raise them clasped,
The juiciness of love revived.

Be generous on this fine day
But do not give all of love
Away.

PART IV
This is How We Say Goodbye

DREAMING

Anecdotes I do not recall,
Moral quandaries unowned and
Faces slapped
On unfamiliar bodies;
Blank mirrors, skyless lakes
Hide reflections, recognition:
I might be sleeping or awake.

I wander in my night head, sometimes sip
From a puddle of consciousness.

CANCER

Death left its calling card for me:
Embossed, embellished, prettified —
As if fine type could hide a date
I did not plan to keep.

It wrote my name in fluid script,
The envelope of linen meant
To tempt my fingers to peel back the seal;
Then left it on my doorstep.

I did not stoop to pick it up —
Ignored the invitation;
I let it lie, let wind, let rain take back the words.
I felt Death step away.

Death left its calling card for me,
It knew my name and number,
It knows my house, my life, my loves;
And knows, someday, I will answer.

There is no need for fancy print
I say to Death: I'll come.
When darkness beckons, I'll be there:
But life is mine, today.

BRACELETS

I wore them
My wrists wrapped in magnets and metal —
Copper and gold, iron and steel;
Blue stones promised strength from infused oil,
Brass and silver to foil the unseen.

Thin wires hugged close blue veins
Beneath sheer white of my skin,
Channeled my rage through threads and charms,
As if powers jangled one against the other
Would ward off harm.

The faces of saints I did not know
Embossed on one strand, a holy field of energy;
The tree of life and Egyptian ankh stamped on others,
Dangling amulets gifted to me
Meant to halt an invasion of rogue cells and doctors.

As I juggled hope, they jingled warnings:
Sound and vibration:
Illusions and delusions
Meant to hold back science that said,
Life is a crapshoot.

Did it matter that even as my arm tingled
Beneath the weight of others' prayers,

I could not believe?
Though love remained
When they fell away, chains released,
I felt only relief.

CLEARING OUT YOUR HOUSE

Stacked on tables, lining shelves
Your photo albums bulged with lives:
Blurred pictures of people we did not know,
Places we had not been.

Each photograph carried, for you,
The taste and scent of who
And what and where of bodies dancing,
Sitting, turned to your camera.
Your eyes knew the before and after
Of moments fixed in time.
We tried to remember what we could not,
Fought over what to do
With what was yours — images
Preserved beneath a shield of plastic.

We could only imagine lives relived,
Laughter reignited, youth reclaimed
When you breathed them whole again
With every turn of well-thumbed pages,
With your finger's every caress.

Left to guess, we closed the covers
As tightly as you had closed your eyes

To us; with utmost care
Guided albums into trash bags,
Dragged them to the curb:
A cruel reminder of what memory is
When it no longer is.

SOME HEARTS ARE

Some hearts are vessels of despair
From the start:
Pinpoints of unhappiness
Embedded in DNA,
Scripts of hopelessness
Inscribed on cells,
Carried in a shattered shell.

What I tell you is, I would
Crack open my chest
If I could dismiss darkness
From within.
Even when tears spill backward
You must see the gash
That passes for a smile
Cut into my face.

APOLOGY

No longer fair of face,
Fine lines and faded hair define years traveled.
Teeth crowd a tightened mouth
And ears cannot hear your wit and mirth:

The mirror mocks what no longer is.
Lips have thinned, skin has sagged
And hips have forgotten
The gentle push of your hands.

You, though, hold my beauty
In your eyes.
When I cry you wash misery
From my face with kisses,
Erase the error of reflection.

Sorrow in this life is tempered
While you are near.

THE QUESTION

How do you let love go
When you have opened the door
To possibility,
When it has strayed into your soul?

Shove it away, palms swept clean,
Face averted from what has been?
Raise your fist, scream and rage,
Heave it, leave it, let it rot?

Do you grind it in the ground,
Feel it squirm beneath your heel?
Break it into bite-sized pieces,
Rip it, tear it, thrash it, smash it,
Brush it off like the pest it has become?

Or should love be ushered out,
The screen door pushed shut gently
Behind that wanderer once welcomed,
As you set the latch?

A GREEDY GOD

It is a greedy god that harvests
Innocent lives, that thrives
On hearts so pure they disappear
Down the gullet of this god
With no thought of holes left in lives
Of others.

It is a selfish god that hoards
What is good, that devours
Unsullied souls, rolls them
Between its greasy palms
With no regard for essence of the future,
Essential beings.

It is a heedless god that desires
The faultless, that crushes perfection,
That wraps a fist about a moment
Rich with potential,
With no concern for what might be,
Who might be.

All that is decent is a feast
For a greedy god.

UKRAINE, 2022

We hear the stories, horrors
Of filth and famine, assault
Of cold and thirst,
Above-ground missiles arced across dark skies,
Wounds left in bricks and bodies.

While we choose wine over water,
Set our teeth to fruit and flesh;
Settle into beds, warm and fed —
Our farewell kisses are not forever.
We shake our heads and watch,
Detached, wonder what is coveted
At any cost.

While we set out flags and wear the colors,
Rage, raise prayers, raise funds
In hopes to ease this anguish,
We contemplate our comfort,
Fear stories that we hear
Are one day ours to tell.

PRAYER, AGAIN

God, Allah, Yahweh, G-d, Higher Power;
Spirit, Mother, Father:
Whatever name we say is insignificant,
As insignificant as supplications of people
You are said to have placed on this planet,
Pledged to love above all things – sparrows will fall
Before we do, in this promise we have heard.
But hear the words we raise —
Skyward —
As if that is where you dwell —
When the Hell we create becomes
Too much
For us to bear and we have to believe there is
Some thing
Some one
Some where
To return us to the pure beings we are at birth.

Whatever name you are called is not important,
Not as important as our belief
That relief is your choice.
Oh, our free will?
That is the punishment with which we must die?
Do not gather to yourself the good,
The innocent, the young;
Gather to yourself those tainted,
Whose souls are tarnished, evil,

Who will not listen, whose hearts are fallow,
Who will not turn swords to plows
Because power is their anchor in this world.

Whatever name you are given
Hear us.
When we turn to you in despair
We are blamed for our humanity
With which you blessed us.
This cannot be thy will on earth
As it is in Heaven.
Deliver us from evil, because temptations
Are too great for us to overcome —
And if you are a Being Supreme,
If you are there,
If God, Allah, Yaweh, G-d, Higher Power;
Spirit, Mother, Father
You can hear us
Let hearts beat with peace;
Release those cursed and return them
To your care.
In your name —
Whatever name you do or do not bear —
We pray.
So be it.

SIXTH GRADE

When your sister died
Our tongues stumbled over what to say.
You returned to the classroom,
Graveyard mud encrusted on your shoes —
You may as well have been
Her ghost.

We looked through you, past you,
Anywhere but at you,
Tried not to notice your mother's neglect:
Tear stains embedded in the blouse
She had not washed nor ironed
And your bare legs, chapped and reddened
In November's chill.

It was an old story, retold every autumn where we lived:
A hunting trip gone awry.
It was three days before they fished her bloated flesh
From the swamp,
Her hunting rifle strapped to her shoulder,
The red vest melted into her chest.
We knew the details.
We were just kids:
We did not know words to ease your pain.
When you laid your head on the desktop
We pretended not to see the weight of your grief.

FUNERAL DAY

I.
This is how we say goodbye:
Long lines snaked through rooms
The color of muted voices;
Idle chatter to ease discomfort;
Awkward memories murmured into shoulders
And hands gripped as if to form a chain
To pull you back from where you lie,
Eyes closed, hands
Precisely placed as they never were;
They should be cupped to hold the tears.

II.
The sanctuary stinks of lilies and regrets.
No open casket we are left to wonder
If this is darkness you desired.
Your soul slips out the cracks in the casket,
Finds its way into the music.

III.
This is our final farewell:
The black hearse snaked through the village
To the hill where you will hear
Each blossom burst, each blade of grass sing.
At the sound of soil falling, we turn aside.
If we stayed, might we hear your laughter?

ACKNOWLEDGMENTS

Without the encouragement of my family and friends, as well as the adept skill of book coach Martha Bullen of Bullen Publishing Services, *Pieces of the World* might have remained pieces on the computer. I am also grateful to Christy Day of Constellation Book Services for her book cover design and beautiful layout of this book.

My longtime friend and former English teacher Lonni Whitchurch has my gratitude for her helpful suggestions as these poems took shape. Her subtle advice nudged my poems into a more reader friendly form, and her recommendations were, as always, spot-on to trouble spots. Thank you, Lonni.

Curtiss Clark was my editor when I was a reporter at *The Newtown Bee*, and has remained my mentor through the years. A magical craftsman with words, his observations as he remarked on the first drafts of my works I took to heart, knowing his thoughtful input would ensure the words I used and images I created were what I truly intended.

A poetry lover and librarian who reads a wide selection of poems, my friend Kim Weber read through *Pieces of the World* as it evolved. Her kind words helped the poetry to emerge in a better way.

Retired English teacher Valerie George has been invaluable as a reader, questioning phrases and grammatical notations, and offering inspiration to continue improving my works. I loved imagining her in her wooded hideaway, pencil in hand, seeking the worthiness in each poem she read. Many thanks for the hours you put into this, Valerie.

Thank you, as well, to Andrea Zimmermann, an author, friend, and librarian, whose sharp eye and way with words pointed out problematic words, phrases, and editing issues. Her input has been valuable as this manuscript took shape.

Did I mention my incredibly patient husband, Phil Crevier? He has put up with my being "in the zone" immersed in my writing, editing, and thoughts when he was talking or trying to attract my attention. He has been my computer troubleshooter, without whom this collection would not have made it off my desk. My first inclination when viruses start yelling at me or frustrating messages hinder my progress is to want to throw the computer through the window. Not a good solution, obviously, and thanks to Phil, not one that ever became a reality.

Phil has also been the first to read or listen to me read aloud a rough draft of these poems, and the first to give a thumbs up or puzzled look that lets me know if I'm on the "write" path. I am so lucky to have the love of this man — and of our children and their spouses, and our granddaughter. The essence of these beloved people inspires poems, even though they may be only fictionalized accounts of moments in time.

I am grateful to all who read my debut book of poetry, *The Peach Quartet and Other Poems*, and all who have attended my readings. My hope is that *Pieces of the World* will be as kindly received, and that those who read this collection will find at least one piece of my world that speaks to them. Thank you, readers.

ABOUT THE AUTHOR

 NANCY K. CREVIER graduated from Bemidji State University in Bemidji, Minnesota with a BA in German in 1978 — the year she also married Philip Crevier and moved to Connecticut, where they raised two wonderful children.

From her childhood in northern Minnesota (where winters are long and temperatures frequently below zero, providing ample opportunity for contemplation) to her adult life transplanted to the East Coast, her poetry has been inspired by people, places, memories, and moments revealed in nature and humanity.

Her debut book of poetry, *The Peach Quartet and Other Poems*, was published in 2022. Nancy has enjoyed sharing poems from this book at readings hosted by many local organizations and through other events. Because writing is a never-ending process, she is happy to introduce her newest collection of poetry, *Pieces of the World*, to readers.

Nancy has co-owned and operated a natural foods restaurant, catered, taught cooking courses, and written food columns. While raising children, she worked part-time at a gardening center and as an educational assistant in the reading department of a local school. She is overjoyed to have the name "Nana" and the title of grandparent added to her resume in recent years.

In 2005, she accepted a position as a reporter at *The Newtown Bee* in Newtown, Connecticut, and went on to become the editor of the newspaper. She retired from *The Newtown Bee* in 2021, and currently lives and writes in Newtown.

To learn more about Nancy, *The Peach Quartet and Other Poems*, and *Pieces of the World*, or to contact Nancy for a book talk or interview, please visit www.ThePeachQuartet.com or email info@thepeachquartet.com.

NOTES

I like to think that my poetry can be as inspiring to others as nature and humanity is for me. These next pages give you space to reflect on Pieces of the World, *or to begin to create your own world of words.*

Made in the USA
Middletown, DE
13 August 2023

36662780R00054